Under the Twelfth Sign

A Play

Enid Coles

A Samuel French Acting Edition

SAMUEL FRENCH

FOUNDED 1830

SAMUELFRENCH-LONDON.CO.UK
SAMUELFRENCH.COM

Copyright © 1989 by Enid Coles
All Rights Reserved

UNDER THE TWELFTH SIGN is fully protected under the copyright laws of the British Commonwealth, including Canada, the United States of America, and all other countries of the Copyright Union. All rights, including professional and amateur stage productions, recitation, lecturing, public reading, motion picture, radio broadcasting, television and the rights of translation into foreign languages are strictly reserved.

ISBN 978-0-573-12276-7

www.samuelfrench-london.co.uk

www.samuelfrench.com

FOR AMATEUR PRODUCTION ENQUIRIES

UNITED KINGDOM AND WORLD EXCLUDING NORTH AMERICA
plays@SamuelFrench-London.co.uk
020 7255 4302/01

Each title is subject to availability from Samuel French,

depending upon country of performance.

CAUTION: Professional and amateur producers are hereby warned that *UNDER THE TWELFTH SIGN* is subject to a licensing fee. Publication of this play does not imply availability for performance. Both amateurs and professionals considering a production are strongly advised to apply to the appropriate agent before starting rehearsals, advertising, or booking a theatre. A licensing fee must be paid whether the title is presented for charity or gain and whether or not admission is charged.

The professional rights in this play are controlled by Samuel French Ltd, 52 Fitzroy Street, London, W1T 5JR.

No one shall make any changes in this title for the purpose of production. No part of this book may be reproduced, stored in a retrieval system, or transmitted in any form, by any means, now known or yet to be invented, including mechanical, electronic, photocopying, recording, videotaping, or otherwise, without the prior written permission of the publisher. No one shall upload this title, or part of this title, to any social media websites.

The right of Enid Coles to be identified as author of this work has been asserted by her in accordance with Section 77 of the Copyright, Designs and Patents Act 1988

CHARACTERS

Mary
David
Miss Samson
Miss Sparrow
Marjorie

The action of the play takes place in Mary's sitting-room

Time—the present

Other plays by Enid Coles
also published by Samuel French Ltd:

Climber
Just a Little Word
Little Benjamin
Once and for All

UNDER THE TWELFTH SIGN

A sitting-room. A winter afternoon

There are two exits, one to the hall, the other to the kitchen. The furniture includes two fireside chairs and a large armchair grouped round a low table. Apart, is a pouffe or stool. US is a writing-table with two unopened envelopes on it. A waste-paper basket is nearby. A few Christmas cards are displayed. David's coat and scarf are thrown over a chair

As the CURTAIN rises, David is standing absolutely motionless, looking at an outspread newspaper. This does not hide the clerical collar he wears with his country suit. Mary enters with a loaded tea-tray. David unfreezes

David Darling, you mustn't. Let me carry that for you. (*He closes the newspaper and puts it behind the cushion of the armchair*)
Mary David, I have to carry trays when you're not here.
David But I am here, today.

Mary puts the tray on the low table

Mary Yes ... Yes, you're here ... today.
David Now will you kindly tell me just what happened.
Mary Let me pour you a cup of tea, first.

They sit at the table. Mary pours and passes a cup which David puts on the table

David Mary, for goodness' sake tell me all about this burglar fellow.
Mary He wasn't really a burglar. He didn't steal anything.
David I'm not bothered about him stealing. It's you I was worried about, my dear darling.
Mary What did you say?
David It's you I was worried about ...
Mary Oh. I thought you said——
David —my dear darling.
Mary (*sentimentally*) Ahh!

David If the blighter had hurt you I'd have beaten the living daylights out of him.

Mary Disgraceful. You—a man of peace?

David Where your safety's concerned, I can soon forget about being peaceful. *What happened?*

Mary Do drink your tea.

With a resigned sigh, David takes a sip of tea and grimaces

You didn't sugar. *(She stands and bustles round to his cup with the sugar-bowl, helps him and stirs the tea)*

David And that just goes to show how I'm feeling. Thank you, darling.

Mary I can't imagine how you heard about it.

David Ah, but then you didn't know I'd called on Mrs Liddicott and Mrs Liddicott's bad leg.

Mary Enough said. And how were they both?

David Her leg's quite dreadful, poor old dear. She insisted on undoing it all and showing me. Again, again.

Mary And Mrs Liddicott, apart from the leg?

David In great spirits. Thrilled to bits to be able to tell me you'd had a burglar.

Mary But where did she get it from?

David Goodness knows. Never stirs from her fireside but she knows everything that goes on in the village.

Mary Everything.

David So having driven home like the clappers, would you very much mind telling me about it?

Mary Well . . . it was really rather amusing.

David Oh, yes. Mrs Liddicott said he was a great big man. Terribly amusing.

Mary I was busy ironing in the kitchen when I thought I heard the front door. I called—but no reply. Waited a moment, expecting you to come trailing through with snow on your shoes . . . *(She gesticulates, sugar-bowl still in hand)*

David Not guilty this time. *(He gently takes the sugar-bowl and returns it to the tray)*

Mary Then—it felt quite cold.

David Your iron? Only another power-cut.

Mary We haven't come to the amusing part yet, David.

The Lights dim slightly

I could hear the grandfather clock ticking in the hall. It sounded different, somehow ... slower ... louder. I was frightened. Then I remembered how I'd coped years ago when we first moved here and I wasn't used to the country.

David Were you frightened then? Why didn't you tell me?

Mary You had quite enough to think about with the new parish. It was just being right out of the village ...

David We could have had a dog. Why didn't I think of it?

Mary I did think of it. We did have a dog.

David We did?

Mary Certainly we did. I imagined a dog for myself. He was a boxer, a big bouncy one. I became very fond of him. After all, he had all the advantages. I had his company but didn't have to take him for walks in the bad weather.

David My poor love. And I thought it was those tablets of the specialist's that did the trick.

Mary No it was Bennie—the boxer. Oh, after a while I got used to being isolated and forgot all about him. But this afternoon I remembered and called "Lie down, Bennie".

David Good for you. Obviously, he was a very large boxer.

Mary Oh, enormous. I was feeling braver by the minute. I called again "*Will* you come here, you brute?"

David And did—er—Bennie do as he was told?

Mary No. He rushed through to your study. I followed, more confident by then. There was a crash and when I went in I found this enormous man lying on the floor shouting "Call this damned boxer off my chest!"

The Lights change

David (*laughing heartily*) Oh, no!

Mary (*sitting*) I do assure you.

David And did you call Bennie off?

Mary Certainly not. I telephoned the police and Bennie stayed on guard until they arrived.

David Well done. But let's get this straight, my darling. This burglar was afraid of your imaginary dog. I don't get it.

Mary Neither did I. But I didn't stop to worry how it worked. I was only too thankful that it did. But when it was all over, I made myself some tea.

David Ah, that's why you're not joining me now.

Mary That's why . . . And I began thinking. David, I have the gift.
David What gift?
Mary You see, being born in March——
David The first of March.
Mary How clever of you to remember.
David Engraved on my heart.
Mary St David's Day. (*She stretches out a hand to David*) You see, I was born for you.
David I'm no saint, darling, (*he presses Mary's hand between his two for a moment*) but thank you for you. (*He relinquishes the hand*) Now, let's start again. You have a gift for something or other because you were born in March.
Mary St David's Day. (*She again stretches out her hand*)
David Now stop it. I have to go off to Leechester to speak to the Mothers' Union, remember?
Mary Pity. Oh, well, don't let them keep you too long.
David From you? Let them just try! Now, this birthday . . .
Mary March birthdays are under the sign of Pisces.
David Never heard of him. He wasn't a saint, for sure.
Mary The twelfth sign . . . of the zodiac . . .

David shakes his head

Didn't they teach you *anything* at theological college?
David Well, not quite that sort of thing, darling.
Mary (*standing*) I'll get my little book and show you.

Mary goes upstage to the writing-table and gets a "destiny in the stars" type of book. David finishes his tea and stands

David I mustn't be late starting off, that snow has made the lane rather tricky.
Mary Here you are. (*She holds out the opened book*) The Twelfth Sign. Pisces, the fishes. Subjects are sensitive, psychic and intuitive.
David (*smiling as he reads*) They can also be confused and temperamental.
Mary (*quickly closing the book*) You're not supposed to read that bit.
David And so?
Mary Well, Mother was born under the twelfth sign as well and she had this extraordinary gift. She always said it would be

passed on to one of the girls—there were two of us. I'm sure I must have told you. By imagining something and concentrating very hard she could persuade anyone it was true.

David In what way?

Mary (*thinking for a moment*) Well, during the war, in our air-raid shelter and scared out of our tiny minds. She convinced us children that we were at the seaside in a beach-hut, sheltering on a rainy day.

David She was just taking your minds off things.

Mary But David, it was so *real*. I could smell the sea, hear the seagulls . . . Then, another time, my sister developed an abscess under a tooth one weekend. She was quite frantic with the pain until Mother said she would take it right away. I can see her now, her fingers clasped, something like this (*she demonstrates*) and concentrating. It worked. Marjorie stopped crying and said it didn't hurt any more. Yet on the Monday, when she was taken to the dentist, he said it was so bad he didn't know how she'd managed to bear it.

David (*impressed in spite of himself*) Amazing!

Mary Mother was an amazing woman. It was the gift. And I've inherited it!

David But I rather think, you know, it was just a coincidence.

Mary Oh, of course. Just a coincidence. Like that great big man being afraid of Bennie the boxer.

David (*defeated*) H'm. Yes, well, we'll talk about it when I get back from the Mothers' Union. (*He looks at his watch*) I really must be off. Now, I've got my notes, haven't I? (*He feels in his jacket pockets, then the inner pockets*) Where did I put them?

Mary (*returning the book to its place*) They're probably in the study. I'll get them for you.

David (*putting on a scarf and picking up his overcoat*) Oh, yes. On my desk. Thank you, darling.

Mary exits to the hall

David stands motionless, his overcoat half on

There is a good pause

Mary (*calling, off*) I can't see them . . . Are you sure you left them in here? David!

Mary enters. As she does so . . .

David moves again, finishes putting on his coat

Your notes aren't in the study.
David You must have moved them.
Mary But I didn't.
David You've been tidying up again. Really, Mary, I do wish you'd leave my things——
Mary Maybe the burglar took them. Maybe *he* wanted to know all about your trip to the Middle East.
David It's not a joke. (*He feels in his pockets in the same order as before. He looks at his watch*) Oh damn, I shall be late. (*He feels down the sides of the chair in which he was sitting*)

Realizing he is really upset, Mary decides to try out her newly-discovered gift. She moves upstage

Mary Er—you didn't put them in the waste-paper basket did you? By mistake?
David Now, if you can't think of anything better than that . . .

Mary picks up the waste-paper basket. Slowly and deliberately she takes out imaginary notes

Mary What are these, then?
David I must be mad. (*He crosses to Mary and takes the notes*)

Mary stares at David's hands, clasping her fingers exactly as she had described her mother's action

Mary (*quietly exultant*) Are they all there?
David (*miming, he looks through the notes*) . . . three, four. Yes, thank you. (*He pockets the notes*) Bless you, you're one in a million.
Mary Yes. Yes, I'm beginning to think I am.
David Now, don't come out, it's bitterly cold. (*He kisses Mary*)
Mary I wish I could come with you.
David No darling, quite impossible. (*He takes his gloves from his pocket*) You stay in the warm . . . with Bennie.
Mary Bye, David, take care now.

David exits to the hall

Mary takes in what has happened. She is happy and confident

I can. I can do it! I just have to use my imagination and

concentrate, as Mother said. How wonderful ... But what a responsibility. It must only be used to help, she always said. Now who can I help?

David enters from the hall

David Some company for you. Lucy Sparrow and Miss Samson are coming up the path.
Mary *Together?*
David They certainly appear to be together.
Mary Impossible. They never speak to each other. Some silly misunderstanding years ago. That little fence between their cottages might be the Berlin Wall.
David Well, I'll let them in and you can see for yourself. Have a nice time! Bye.

David exits to the hall

Mary crosses to the tea-tray and replaces David's cup on it

Miss Samson enters, rosy-cheeked and bringing the fresh air in with her. She wears an anorak and jersey with trousers tucked into big boots

Miss Samson Hello, Mary, old thing. Surprise, surprise!
Mary And a very nice one, Sammy. I'm so pleased to see you——

Miss Sparrow enters, wearing a tweed coat and a headscarf. Her stockinged feet emphasize the difference in height of the visitors

—both!

Miss Samson and Miss Sparrow pointedly ignore each other

Miss Sparrow Hello, I've taken my boots off. Mustn't put snow on your pretty carpet.
Mary Hello, Lucy. Let me take your coat. (*She helps her off with her coat*)
Miss Sparrow Thank you. It's beautifully warm in here.
Miss Samson (*removing her coat and throwing it on the chairback*) Goodness, Mary, it's hot in here. Stuffy after outside.
Miss Sparrow Beautifully warm. I think it's been colder than ever today. (*She takes off her headscarf and pats her hair*)
Miss Samson You ought to be out, Mary old thing, it's a glorious day for walking. I tramped over the moor, absolutely marvel-

lous. Didn't meet a soul ... until I reached your gate. (*She stomps round the room, looking at the Christmas cards*)

Miss Sparrow My brother gave me a lift in his pick-up truck. He was taking feed up to the sheep and I said "Mary must be lonely out there, I'll go with you and tell her all the village news."

Miss Samson Mind you, I haven't any village gossip for you. Don't indulge in that sort of thing.

Mary (*between them and determined to do her best*) What a walker you are, Sammy ... Any signs of the lambing starting, Lucy?

Miss Sparrow Fairly soon after Christmas, Leonard says. I shall look forward to seeing them ... when it's a bit warmer.

Miss Samson I shall probably walk even further tomorrow. Take a look at Leonard Sparrow's ewes.

Miss Sparrow Baby lambs are so pretty.

Miss Samson Won't be long before they're on someone's plates.

Miss Sparrow Leonard's picking me up on his way back, I haven't got long.

Mary Perhaps you could take Miss Samson back with you?

Miss Sparrow Who? Oh ...! Oh, no, the cab only holds two.

Miss Samson Mary, you know me. Ride in something like a smelly old pick-up when I could be walking?

Mary But it gets dark so early.

Miss Samson I'll be all right.

Miss Sparrow *She'll* be quite safe!

Mary Well, come along, both of you. Sit down and be comfortable. (*She picks up Miss Samson's coat*)

Miss Sparrow sits in the armchair. Miss Samson takes the seat furthest from her, the pouffe, and sits with her back to the audience

I'll just put these out in the hall.

Mary exits

Miss Samson and Miss Sparrow sit motionless. There is a pause

Mary returns and the visitors unfreeze

Oh dear, Sammy, wouldn't you like a bigger seat?

Miss Sparrow (*as if to herself*) The one she's got is quite big enough.

Mary Something with a back?

Miss Samson Thank you, but *my* back doesn't have to be sup-
ported.
Mary Do sit here. (*She indicates the chair next to Miss Sparrow*)
Miss Samson If it makes you feel happier . . . (*She hauls herself up
from the low seat*)
Miss Sparrow Oh, well, if her back doesn't need support . . . (*She
takes the cushion from the chair indicated and tucks it behind her
own back*)

Miss Samson, with a glare, sits in the cushionless chair

Mary Now I'll get you both a drink.
Miss Samson Jolly good idea.
Mary (*picking up the tea-tray*) I'm sure you're ready for a cup of
tea.
Miss Samson Ah . . . ! Not quite so jolly.
Miss Sparrow Not for me, thank you, I had a cup of tea with my
brother before we set off. (*She giggles*) In fact, I had *two*!
Miss Samson What mad, impulsive little creatures some people
are!
Mary Not tea, then. How about a glass of something?
Miss Samson Now you're talking.

*Mary places the tea-tray on the writing-table. Comfortable in their
armchairs, Miss Samson and Miss Sparrow don't see Mary smile to
herself as she decides to try out her newly-discovered gift. Miming,
with exaggerated movements, she wipes a bottle and places two
glasses (all imaginary). NB: All stage directions which refer to the
wine are, of course, mimed*

Nothing like a glass of something on a day like this.
Mary The bottle had a cobweb on it.
Miss Samson Sounds promising, old thing.

Mary comes downstage with the two glasses

Mary There. My home-made elderflower.
Miss Samson Not so promising.
Miss Sparrow Oh no, *thank* you, not for me.
Mary We've nothing else, I'm afraid.

Rather reluctantly, the glasses are accepted. Intensely, Mary watches, clasping her fingers exactly as before. Miss Samson sips tentatively

Miss Sparrow What a pretty colour. (*She drains her glass in one*) That—is—delicious! (*She tilts back her head for the last few drops*) Ab—sol—utely delicious!
Mary (*fetching the bottle*) Good. Try another.
Miss Sparrow Oh, I mustn't. I never do.
Mary Just to keep out the cold.
Miss Sparrow No, really, I think not.
Mary Very well. (*She turns away*)
Miss Sparrow (*to herself*) Mustn't be uncivil, Lucy. Rude about Mary's delicious wine. (*To Mary*) Just a little one, please.
Mary (*turning back*) Right. You say "when".

Mary refills Miss Sparrow's glass; she pours slowly and once stops with an enquiring look. But Miss Sparrow, smiling, is gazing away. Mary continues pouring and her expression tells us the glass is nearly full. Miss Sparrow's hand trembles a little, obviously the wine has overflowed

Miss Sparrow *When!* Oh dear, very sorry.
Mary Don't worry. I'll get some kitchen paper.
Miss Sparrow Oh, no. Such a pity to waste it. (*With her forefinger, she wipes along the base, up the stem and round the bowl of her glass with great concentration. She then licks the finger appreciatively*)
Miss Samson Aren't you drinking, Mary?
Mary No, somehow I don't think it would do *me* much good. (*She sits*)
Miss Samson Not feeling under the weather, are you? You look a bit peaky to me.
Miss Sparrow Mary, did I tell you I think that you're looking very well and pretty today. And I love your glass, too. Very pretty.
Mary I'm glad you like them. (*She is elated at the success of her experiment*)

Miss Samson's sips are no longer tentative. Miss Sparrow is feeling the effect of her two quick drinks. This manifests itself in a deliberation of her speech, rather than the conventional slur

Miss Sparrow (*holding up her glass*) Most unusual. Come to think

of it, I don't think I've seen a glass quite like this one ever
before.

Mary I don't suppose you have.

Miss Sparrow Have you had them long?

Mary Er—no, not very long at all. In fact, this is the very first time
I've ever used them.

Miss Sparrow Ooh, aren't I honoured?

Miss Samson Very decent of you, Mary, to let me christen them.
But it isn't the glass that counts. It's the stuff inside. And this is
jolly good. (*She holds out her glass for refill*)

Mary Thank you. (*She fills Miss Samson's glass*)

Miss Samson No. Thank *you*. (*She drinks half*) Really good, I
mean. No humbug.

Miss Sparrow (*with a sniff*) That makes a change.

Miss Samson Did somebody say something?

Miss Sparrow I said—I said it makes a change. To have a little
drink, I mean. (*She giggles*) I'm not used to it.

Miss Samson Obviously. (*She drains her glass and with a great
sweeping gesture holds it out for more*) I have never tasted home-
made wine quite like this before.

Mary (*filling Miss Samson's glass*) No?

Miss Samson No! Are you sure it's all your own making?

Mary Oh, entirely my own.

Miss Samson What a gift.

Mary Yes, it's a gift. A special gift my mother passed on to me.

Miss Sparrow (*swaying*) The room's going to and fro ... to and
fro ...

Miss Samson What a strong head some people don't have. My
dear Miss Sparrow ...

Miss Sparrow Do call me Lucy.

Miss Samson How do you do, Lucy, I'm Sammy.

*Miss Samson solemnly extends a hand to Miss Sparrow who
carefully changes her glass from right hand to left and then shakes
hands*

Miss Sparrow I am very pleased to meet you.

Miss Samson We ought to become acquainted, you and I.

Miss Sparrow I will call on you when I am out riding on my
bicycle.

Miss Samson Do that. I live at number six, Church Lane.

Miss Sparrow Oh, that will make a lovely little ride ... I live at number seven. (*Swaying and waving her headscarf*) To and fro ...

Miss Samson Stand up and take a little walk round.

Miss Sparrow (*carefully replacing her glass on the table, clutching the arms of the chair*) Do you think it will help?

Miss Samson Try it and see. Just a little walk round.

Miss Sparrow Just—a—little—round—walk. (*She stands and foolishly, headscarf in hand, does a complete turn on the spot*) Oh yes, that's better (*She sits abruptly*) I think.

Miss Samson Thank you, Mary, I won't say no.

Miss Samson holds out her glass. Mary fills it, then tops up Miss Sparrow's glass, on the table. Miss Sparrow, meticulously folding her headscarf, manages not to notice

Mary Do either of you know anything about the stars?

Miss Sparrow Stars? Oh, yes. I can see them. All over the place!

Mary The zodiac, I mean.

Miss Samson Didn't know you were interested in motorcars, Mary, old thing. My old bus was a Zodiac, she went like a bomb.

Mary The twelve signs of the zodiac. Aries, Taurus ... (*She moves upstage, still concentrating*)

Miss Sparrow Twelve. What a pretty number. I think that twelve is the prettiest number I know. (*She looks at her full glass*) Who did that? Oh, well ... tidy it up, Lucy. (*She drinks*)

The Lights very gradually dim as the afternoon's light fades

Miss Samson Twelve ... There are twelve hours in a day, if that's any use to you.

Miss Sparrow And twelve hours in a night.

Miss Samson Clever little Lucy. Twelve hours in a night as well. (*Taking great care with the pronunciation*) What an extraordinary coincidence

Miss Sparrow And there were twelve—um—disciples.

Miss Samson And twelve in a jury. "Twelve good men and true." Twelve men, what a splendid thought.

Miss Sparrow (*with a sigh*) Yes, indeed. We could do with them in the village.

Miss Samson I'll share them with you, Lucy. You can have six of
my good men.
Miss Sparrow And true. That's very generous of you, Sammy . . .
And twelve days of Christmas . . .
Miss Samson Just imagine, *five* gold rings!

Miss Samson and Miss Sparrow gradually change to singing

Miss Sparrow Four calling birds
Miss Samson Three French hens
Miss Sparrow Two turtle doves. (*With alcoholic sentimentality*)
Ahh!
Miss Sparrow \ (*together, in excruciating harmony*) And a par-
Miss Samson ∫   tridge in a peartree.

They laugh together, pleased with themselves

Mary Do excuse me a moment, I must just look at my casserole.
Miss Sparrow Of course. Got to be ready for the hungry worker.
Miss Samson It must be rather nice to have someone to cook for,
to have someone returning.
Miss Sparrow Oh, poor little Sammy. Tell you what, come and
have supper with us this evening.
Miss Samson Steady now. What would your brother say to that?
Miss Sparrow He'd love it. He admires you very much. Says that
you're a fine figure of a woman!
Miss Samson Bless my soul! I wish I'd known that years ago. (*She
scratches her head, rubs her cheek or some characteristic gesture
that will show well in the ensuing freeze*)

Miss Sparrow leans forward to put down her glass on the table

Mary I won't be long.

Mary exits to the kitchen

The visitors freeze

Marjorie (*off, from the hall*) Mary, where are you?

*Marjorie enters from the hall. She wears a warm coat and boots,
and carries an "organizer" handbag*

Marjorie Haven't you got the strength to switch the light on? (*She presses the light switch*)

The Lights come on. She looks around the room and through the occupants, then crosses towards the kitchen

(*Calling*) Mary!
Mary (*off; calling*) Hello, Marjorie, get warm. I'm just coming.

Marjorie puts her handbag on the table, removes her coat and slings it on Samson's chair, half-draping her. Miss Samson and Miss Sparrow remain frozen

Marjorie (*calling*) Do you know what time the carol concert is? I'd rather like to put in an appearance.
Mary (*off; calling*) Is it in the local rag? It's there somewhere.

Marjorie looks around for the newspaper and finds it behind the cushion of Miss Sparrow's chair

Marjorie OK. Found it. (*She wanders about, rustling through the newspaper. For a moment, it seems that she will sit down in the chair Miss Samson occupies, but at the last moment she changes her mind as she finds the article. Calling*) Yes, here it is. Seven o'clock. It'll be a bit of a rush. I'll go and tidy myself now while you rustle up the food. (*She collects her coat, slings down the paper and crosses the hall*)

Mary enters from the kitchen, oven-cloth in hand

Miss Sparrow and Miss Samson begin to unfreeze

Mary Marjorie . . .
Marjorie (*about to exit, not turning*) Yes?
Mary Leonard Sparrow wasn't at the gate, was he?
Marjorie No, not a soul for miles. Press on with that meal, can you?

Marjorie exits to the hall

Mary Sorry about that. Marjorie never was very sociable.
Miss Sparrow It didn't trouble me. Nothing seems to trouble me this afternoon.
Miss Samson You and your sister aren't a bit alike, old thing.
Mary Not one scrap. That's often the way.

Miss Samson Well, I must be starting back. (*She stands*) It's quite
  a step.
Miss Sparrow Oh, but you must come back with Leonard and me.
Miss Samson But won't that be a bit of a squeeze?
Miss Sparrow Maybe. But Leonard will like that.
Miss Samson I shan't mind it myself, to be honest.
Mary It's been so good to have you both here. I've enjoyed your
  company ... Listen!

NB: There is no noise

Miss Sparrow There's my big brother. (*She stands with great care*)
Miss Samson Oh, I feel all girlish again. Many thanks, Mary, I
  can recommend the cellar.
Mary Come again. We've lots more, just the same. Your coats are
  in the hall, keeping warm by the radiator.
Miss Sparrow (*kissing Mary*) Thank you, Mary, for your wonderful hospi— hospital—(*She shakes her head*) That's not right.
Miss Samson (*taking Miss Sparrow's arm*) Lucy means your
  elderflower wine.

  Mary, Miss Sparrow and Miss Samson exit to the hall

There is a slight pause

  *Marjorie enters from the hall without a coat. She crosses to the
  writing-table and opens the two envelopes*

  Mary enters from the hall, shivering slightly and rubbing her arms

Marjorie There's a card from Rosemary Brown. Did we remem-
  ber her?
Mary Yes, I sent one.
Marjorie Oh, good ... What a helluva day. (*She sets out the cards
  with the others*)
Mary It's been a wonderful day. Marjorie, I must tell you. I have
  the gift. I found out this afternoon.
Marjorie (*turning quickly*) You found out *what*?
Mary You know that Mother always said that one of us would
  inherit the gift.
Marjorie Yes, she said that, all right.
Mary Well, it's me. I have it.
Marjorie And what makes you think that?
Mary I've actually been using it. I did just what Mother said.

Imagined something myself then concentrated really hard. (*Automatically, her fingers clasp for a moment*) And they were quite convinced.

Marjorie Who are "they"?

Mary All of them. Well, the last time, Lucy Sparrow and Sammy. I made them friends again.

Marjorie How on earth did you manage that?

Mary Got them drinking together, they were really merry.

Marjorie But there's nothing in the house. *That* will have to be rectified before Christmas.

Mary But—don't you see? I gave them *imaginary* elderflower wine! I do wish you'd heard them singing "The Twelve Days of Christmas" in so-called harmony. The first attempt at harmony for ten years.

Marjorie (*amused*) When was this?

Mary Just before you came in. You must have noticed how mellow they were.

A tiny pause

Marjorie But I didn't see them.

Mary Oh, of course you saw them. They were sitting here. (*She indicates*)

Marjorie My dear sister, granted that I may possibly have missed the Sparrow, I could hardly avoid seeing Miss Samson.

Mary ... I don't understand.

Marjorie Are you feeling all right? You remembered to take your tablets, didn't you?

Mary Of course I remembered. I feel wonderful. So would you if you had the gift.

Marjorie (*sardonically*) *If!*

Mary I helped David, too, when he mislaid the notes for his lecture.

Marjorie David?

Mary I gave him some totally imaginary ones. He went off to Leechester with them quite happily.

Marjorie *David?*

Mary My poor darling, the Mothers' Union always gets him into a state. You'd think by now he'd be used to speaking in public.

Marjorie Oh, David speaks in public?

Mary Clergymen usually do, you know. It's a little habit they have.

Marjorie I see. He's a clergyman.

Mary Of course he's a clergyman. Are *you* feeling all right?

Marjorie So you're calling the Vicar your "poor darling"?

Mary Surely I can call my husband what I like? Marjorie, you're being rather odd.

Marjorie Sit down, dear. (*She leads Mary to a chair*) Mary, you and the Vicar aren't married. Yes, I know you've been keen on him for years. And I'm afraid they all know that in the village, as well.

Mary Have you the nerve to say that David and I are living together?

Marjorie Not for one moment. He lives at the vicarage with his old mum. And you live here—with me.

Mary But—oh, that's nonsense. Why, he was here for tea. (*She stands and moves upstage to the tray on the writing-table*) Here's the tray.

Marjorie Yes, with only one cup.

Mary David's.

Marjorie Yours ... Mary, nobody's been here. Nobody at all. There are no footsteps in the snow. Not the Vicar's, not Miss Samson's, not even little Miss Sparrow's.

Mary And not the burglar's?

Marjorie A burglar, now, as well! No, not the burglar's.

Mary Are you saying that I'm suffering from delusions?

Marjorie Of course not. You've simply got a powerful imagination. I can't think why you don't write a book or something. Put it to some use.

Mary But I did put it to some use. I helped people with it, as Mother always said.

Marjorie People? Which people? Oh, you helped someone, I do realize ... yourself. Look, you're alone too much. It's a pity I have to keep on my job, but there it is. I go out so early and it's a long day for you.

Mary Don't look so worried. I'm not a bit lonely. I have masses of people in and out all day.

The Lights dim slightly

(*With tragic realization*) I don't ... do I?

Marjorie (*shaking her head*) You can't expect people to come all
the way out here . . .

Mary But they were so vivid. They *were* here. I'm sure they were.
And David . . .

David (*off*) It's you I was worried about, my dear darling. If the
blighter had touched you I'd have beaten the living daylights
out of him . . . The first of March . . . engraved on my heart . . .
Thank you for you, Mary.

Mary listens in anguish

Marjorie Up that awful lane in this weather . . . Mary!

Mary M'm?

Marjorie What's the matter?

Mary I was listening . . .

Marjorie I should hope you were. I was speaking to you.

Mary Not listening to you. Oh, David . . .

Marjorie You're thoroughly run-down. Look, I'll try to get some
leave and take you away for a few days.

Mary So I haven't got the gift.

Marjorie How would you like to go to London? A complete
change. Stay in one of those new hotels? Go to the theatre?

Mary I haven't got the gift . . . But Mother had——

Marjorie She certainly had. I can remember that awful toothache
as if it were yesterday. It was agony, yet she imagined it right
away.

Mary —and she swore that she'd pass it on to one of us girls.

Marjorie Maybe she did.

Mary Said it when she was dying . . . What did you say?

Marjorie Maybe she did pass it on. But not to you.

Mary But I was the closest to her. I was born under the twelfth
sign, like her.

Marjorie Yes, and remember my birthday?

Mary Of course. The twenty-ninth of February, leap-year day.

Marjorie And you know what that means?

Mary That you only get a real birthday once every four years,
poor love.

Marjorie Granted. But think how young it keeps me! Does it
mean anything else?

Mary (*becoming irritated*) Only that I shall have to start saving up
again for your birthday directly Christmas is over.

Marjorie Anything else?
Mary I don't think so, no. Why should it?
Marjorie But it does means that I, too, was born under the twelfth
sign, Pisces.
Mary You? "Sensitive and psychic"? (*A little laugh in which the
tears aren't far away*) Are you joking?
Marjorie Ludicrous, isn't it?
Mary You think that *you* inherited the gift?
Marjorie Could be.
Mary (*tearfully*) Then why don't you use it? Help somebody with
it, as Mother used to do?
Marjorie Maybe I do use it, sometimes. On you, for instance.
Mary I don't believe you.
Marjorie No, I didn't expect you to.
Mary No. I should realize. Even if I haven't got the gift myself . . .
I should know what you were up to.
Marjorie Of course you would.
Mary You couldn't fool me.

*Marjorie smiles enigmatically. Mary doesn't see this, she is feeling in
her pocket, unsuccessfully, for a handkerchief. She rubs her hand
over her wet cheeks*

Marjorie Oh, for goodness' sake mop up and let's have our meal
before it's completely spoiled.
Mary You carry on. I don't want anything. (*She rubs her face with
her hand*)
Marjorie Can't you find a handkerchief?
Mary (*shaking her head, sniffing*) I'll go upstairs and get one. In
fact, if you don't mind, I'll stay up there.
Marjorie No, don't go upstairs, my dear, it's so cold. Here, why
don't you use my spare? (*She opens her handbag on the table.
Slowly and deliberately she takes out an imaginary handkerchief.
Unfolding this, she passes it to Mary*)
Mary Thank you, Marjorie. (*She dries her cheeks but is still very
tearful*) I was feeling so well and happy. Happier than I've felt
for years . . . Why did you have to spoil it all?

*Marjorie realizes what she has done. She nods, ruefully. We see her
come to a decision. Moving slightly away from Mary, she stares
hard over her head at a spot just inside the room from the hall.*

Clasping her fingers, exactly as Mary did formerly, she concentrates. After a moment, Mary looks at her

I said, "Why did you have to spoil it all?" (*A pause*) Marjorie, whatever's the matter? (*She stands*) Why are you staring like that? (*Turning, she follows Marjorie's gaze to the spot*)

The Lights flood

(*With complete conviction*) David! (*She moves towards the spot; joyfully*) Oh, David, darling, you're back again!

CURTAIN

FURNITURE AND PROPERTY LIST

Only essential items as mentioned in the text are listed below. Further dressing may be added at the producer's discretion.

On stage: Writing-table. *On it:* two unopened Christmas cards, astrology book
Low table
Waste-paper basket
Armchair. *On it:* cushion
2 chairs. *On them:* cushions, **David**'s coat and scarf
Pouffe
Newspaper for **David**

Off stage: Tray. *On it:* teapot, cup and saucer, milk-jug, sugar-bowl **(Mary)**
Handbag **(Marjorie)**

Personal: **David:** watch, gloves in coat pocket
Sparrow: headscarf

LIGHTING PLOT

Property fittings required: overhead lamp
Interior. The same scene throughout

<table>
<tr><td colspan="2">To open: Winter afternoon light</td><td></td></tr>
<tr><td>Cue 1</td><td>Mary: "... the amusing part yet, David."
Reduce lighting</td><td>(Page 2)</td></tr>
<tr><td>Cue 2</td><td>Mary: "... damned boxer off my chest!"
Revert to original lighting</td><td>(Page 3)</td></tr>
<tr><td>Cue 3</td><td>Sparrow: "... tidy it up, Lucy." (She drinks)
Gradually reduce lighting</td><td>(Page 12)</td></tr>
<tr><td>Cue 4</td><td>Marjorie presses the light switch on
Snap on overhead lamp and covering spot</td><td>(Page 14)</td></tr>
<tr><td>Cue 5</td><td>Mary: "... people in and out all day."
Reduce lighting</td><td>(Page 17)</td></tr>
<tr><td>Cue 6</td><td>Mary follows Marjorie's gaze
The Lights flood</td><td>(Page 20)</td></tr>
</table>

EFFECTS PLOT

No cues

www.ingramcontent.com/pod-product-compliance
Ingram Content Group UK Ltd.
Pitfield, Milton Keynes, MK11 3LW, UK
UKHW021819150726
7214IPUK00017B/210